Ellwood Haines Stokes

Starlets by the Sea

Ellwood Haines Stokes

Starlets by the Sea

ISBN/EAN: 9783337033699

Printed in Europe, USA, Canada, Australia, Japan

Cover: Foto ©ninafisch / pixelio.de

More available books at **www.hansebooks.com**

STARLETS

BY THE SEA.

Rev. E. H. STOKES, D.D.

"One Star differeth from another Star,
in glory."

OCEAN GROVE, N. J.
1895.

AFTER

NEARLY HALF A CENTURY OF HAPPY WEDDED LIFE,

IT IS A SUPREME PLEASURE TO

DEDICATE

THIS LITTLE VOLUME TO

MY BELOVED WIFE

AS A

SLIGHT TESTIMONIAL OF MY HIGH APPRECIATION OF HER PATIENT

TOIL, HELPFUL WORDS, AND CHEERFUL SMILES ALL ALONG

THE LENGTHENED WAY; AND MINGLED WITH THESE

APPRECIATIONS, ARE BLESSED ANTICIPATIONS

OF ETERNAL FELLOWSHIP

IN HEAVEN.

CONTENTS.

INTRODUCTORY.

THE collection contained in the following pages, is called STARLETS, because of the brevity of the articles, and their inconspicuousness in the literary firmament—little stars, scarcely discernable by the unaided vision ;—scattered, almost nothing, but gathered, may become illuminated haze, like the milky way, or, if the intellectual telescope is brought to bear steadily upon them, the nebula may unfold in such electric glow, as will attract some wanderer's eye, or, possibly cheer some sad and lonely heart. Most of them had their inception and inspiration in sight and sound of God's great Ocean :—hence, Starlets By the Sea.

They have been written at various times and for various purposes. Some, are little tributes to departed friends, still fondly loved ; a few are for the living ; others, to point a moral, introduce a book, or break the tediousness of an annual report. Still others, to grace the felicity of a marriage, or perchance, soothe the sorrows of a stricken heart. May the smile of God, like the small rain on the tender herb, be upon them.

The dates affixed, simply refer to the year when written. Nothing more.   E. H. S.

REV. CHARLES PITMAN. D.D.

I.

HE spoke ! the voice was soft and clear,
  Like liquid silver's softest flow.
He spoke ! all ears were bent to hear,
  As lute of Orpheus long ago.
He spoke ! and hardened hearts were rent,
  Like Horeb's rock by Moses' rod.
He spoke ! and human hearts were blent
  In holiest union with God.

II.

O holy man of matchless might,
  Who swayed for God each gathered host,
Swayed them in love's supreme delight,
  As men were moved at Pentecost.
" Who, who is this," the stranger cried,
  " Whose flame like light flies everywhere?"
A thousand loving hearts replied,
  And " Pitman !" murmured through the air.

1878.

THE OLD MINISTERS.

I.

ONE night in Venice, soft and clear,
    When stars were out in grand parade,
Just at my door, a gondolier
    Stopped, and celestial music made ;
I stood entranced, then bowing down,
    The currents of my soul were strong ;
Music, white-robed, wore golden crown,
    And breathed the eloquence of song.

II.

And so our own Bartine is here,
    He wields divine magician's rod,
More than Venetian gondolier,
    He trills the eloquence of God.
Eyes, lips and tongue, flow lofty speech,
    From Sinai's unto Calvary's height ;
His themes are limitless in reach,
    And, sunlike, flame with heaven's light.

III.

Exalted saints ! whose union sweet,
    Blended the human with divine ;
Lowly ye sat at Jesus' feet,
    Then, Alp-like, rose to the sublime.
O mountain saints ! Sometimes the night
    Gathered about your weary feet ;
No matter ! crowns of living light
    Enwreathed each honored brow complete.

1889.

REV. JOHN P. DURBIN. D. D.

I.

DEEP midnight reigns! the storm is high,
    There's terror on the awful deep.
Fierce lightnings blaze! the vaulted sky
    Howls with the angry tempest's sweep.
Behold, a wreck! a hundred lives
    Without a prayer, without a groan,
Lover and maiden, husbands, wives,
    Sink voiceless into depths unknown.

II.

A hundred more! See, hurry, fly!
    Cling wildly to the broken mast.
The life-boat! hear the distant cry,
    And hope survives the midnight blast.
I seem to see it, hear it all,
    The broken ship, the midnight cry;
High eloquence holds carnival,
    For Durbin speaks with lips and eye

1878.

SACRED ORATORY.

I.

NOW Winner comes, sedate and slow,
  Then, flashes out, a meteor bold ;
A brilliant star, with steady glow,
  A warrior, with his helmet gold ;
A mountain, mid the rising hills,
  A lofty cone, with crown of snow ;
A river swollen by the rills,
  A HUDSON, in majestic flow.

II.

Truth found new lustre at his hands,
  His fire-touched tongue with wisdom flows ;
Wrong halted at his high commands,
  And right, emancipated, rose.
His words were zigzag lightning wrath,
  His voice the angry tempest's roar ;
Then, soft as summer zephyr's path,
  And lo ! we weep, obey, adore.

III.

A royal race, high pedigree—
  Born of the skies, and thither bound ;
Still wider your success shall be,
  And grander all your work be crowned :
Go forth ! Nor falter ! Earth is wide,
  Unfold, enlarge, turn every sod ;
Your banner is the Crucified,
  Your leader, the Eternal God.

1889.

REV. ALFRED COOKMAN.

I.

HUSH ! hush ! there's silence in the air,
    There's sacredness beneath our feet,
  And tender are the tones of prayer,
    While rainbows girt the mercy-seat.
  'Tis Cookman pleads, nor pleads in vain,
    Leading a soul to joys above.
  Oh for such saintliness again,
    Paulinic faith, Johannic love !

II.

We miss thee, Cookman, whose mild eye
    Brought hope where nothing could console ;
  We bless thee for the gospel cry
    Which brought salvation to the soul.
  We miss thee ! yet we miss thee not,
    Thy absence is the Father's will,
  And if so e'er we mourn our lot,
    Thy saintly spirit cheers us still.

1878.

SILVER TONES.

I.

LUTE on summer's moonlit lake,
  A soft and silver lute, afar ;
Its tones the tenderest memories wake,
  The tender tones of Whitecar.
Then towering like the eagle's flight,
  Which cloudward, sunward, starward rise ;
He plumes his wings in liquid light,
  And perches mid the glowing skies.

II.

Hail, Whitecar, of silver tongue !
  For truth, "the golden mouth," to-day,
His speech, like old Chrysostom's, rung,
  And through the soul has royal sway.
And Jefferis, too, young, graceful, fair,
  While in his Master's work succeeds,
Where duty called, was promptly there,
  With gentle words and kindly deeds.

III.

Young men ! your fathers toiled of yore :
  Their day was iron, but your's is gold ;
Your times unfolding more and more,
  You should excel a thousand fold.
Learning is now a river's flow,
  And science a potential rod ;
The world with wealth is all aglow ;
  Go forth and capture it for God !

1889.

REV. SAMUEL Y. MONROE. D.D.

I.

O MAN of God! My brother, thou,
  With spirit draped, and tear-dew'd eyes—
I tremble, and before thee bow,
  And seem to join thee in the skies.
A granite base, a lofty spire,
  Both blending gracefully in one,
Symmetrical, still rising higher,
  A meteor, and then a sun!

II.

Amid the lights—electric glow!
  Amid the hills—an Alpine height;
Out from the streams—like ocean's flow—
  He widened towards the infinite:
And yet he stooped to kiss the child,
  He plead for right against the wrong;
A crash! a groan! a shudder wild!
  And life *was an unfinished song.*

1890.

THE ALL SEEING EYE.

THROUGH all the midnight sky,
　　Wailing tempests sweep ;
　Watched by the All Seeing Eye,
　　Storm-tossed birds may sleep.

1885.

SOLITUDE.

NO eye beholds me !　In this solitude,
　　I stand alone.　The sky, the sea, the air,
Seem vacant all ; yet the enduring good—
　God, the All Father, He is everywhere ;
He sees, He knows—and though my friends have fled,—
Speaks to my soul, and I am comforted.

1886.

THE FAMILY ALTAR.

AH ! do not turn away with thoughtless gaze,
　　From this sweet scene of gentleness and love :
In tender accents the fond father prays,
　And softly fall rich blessings from above :
The prayer has touched the secret source of joy,
And bliss supreme is found in the divine employ.

1886.

REV. JOHN S. INSKIP.

WHO shall the glad'ning glory now unfold?
  Who shall the splendors of the scene rehearse?
Earth's grandeur multiplied a thousand fold,--
  Transfigured world, joy's widening universe ;
Compounded bliss, raptures unmeasured, given
To thee, thou two years, with the Lord, in heaven.

Thou two years with the Lord ! Unfathomed deeps
  Of matchless love, which ransomed from the fall,—
Traversed by thee—a love which never sleeps ;
  Then, rising heights transcendant, visions fall
On thee, beyond all human language, bright,
Each like their Author, God, the Infinite.

Oh, that I had some new expanse of thought,
  Some new and God-coined words such thoughts to show:
Some glints of glory all divinely wrought,
  To set this fragmentary song aglow ;
Yet, had I all, how poor, alas, to thee,
Whose glory widens on eternally !

1886.

MOUNTAINS.

STUPENDOUS piles of majesty and might,
    Whose sides reveal the untamed tempest's wrath,
And dark ravines unfold destruction's path,
Leading far down to deeper shades of night ;
Where torrents rush and roar in wild delight,
Whose tops are kissed by morning's dewy light,
Or, tipped by sun-glow at the close of day ;
Rent, torn, wrath-marked, in such a human way,
Ye seem like brothers in this human fray.
Sometimes ye smile, then robed in darkness, frown ;
Now green and jubilant, then bare and brown ;
Silent and solemn, or in gladness gay ;
Low at your feet we learn how to endure,
And through earth's storms eternal life secure.

1891.

SNOWY SAILS.

WINDS gaily blow,
    Waves brightly flow,—
Sun-tipped with splendor as onward they go ;
        Sails snowy white,
        Flash in the light,
Beauty is smiling with gladness aglow.

1891.

CLING AND SING.

STILL, more closely let me cling,
    To Thy loving heart and hand ;
Still more cheerfully I sing,
        Passing through Immanuel's land.

1890.

THE OUTLOOK.

I.

RING the bells of the olden times ;
   Ring bells of many years ago ;
Ring out the bells in joyous chimes,
   And let the mellow rhythm flow !
Ring softly, bells of holy joy,
   Ring solemn bells, the past unfold ;
Ring silver bells, hopes bright employ,
   And love, ring richer bells of gold.

II.

I stand upon Time's lofty mount,
   And trill my song, a trembling lay ;
Ancient and modern, I recount,
   The earlier and the latter day.
I scan the dark horizon's rim,
   My spirit cries, " What of the night ? "
" The morning cometh ! " but so dim,
   There scarcely gleams a ray of light.

III.

I look and wonder, watch and wait,
   When will the gloomy night be past ?
Who will unbar the golden gate,
   And let the morning in at last ?
I wait, and watch, and strain my eyes,
   And lift to God my fervent prayer ;
When lo ! along the solemn skies
   A glint of sunlight, faint and fair !

1889.

"ON JOYFUL WING."

"ON joyful wing!" Arise, and sing,
  Ye song birds of the soul ;
Through mount and vale let songs prevail,
  And where the billows roll ;
Go forth, "On joyful wing,"
  Sing, sing, O sing,
Through all the world, forever,
  Let widening echoes ring.

" On joyful wing!" Haste, haste to bring,
  High tributes of the soul ;
And lay them low, with love aglow,
  Where songs eternal roll ;
Go forth, " On joyful wing,"
  Sing, sing, O sing,
And crown with royal gladness
  Your own *Immortal King*.

1886.

RADIANT SONGS.

RADIANT with light the bending skies,
  With radiant hope earth is aglow ;
And joy to radiant joy replies,
  As skies resmile in lakes below.

So radiant hearts to hearts unfold,
  So radiant hope keeps life aflame ;
So " Radiant Songs," the heart's best gold,
  Shall gladden earth with Jesus' name.

1891.

REV. GEORGE W. BATCHELDER, A. M.

YES ; I remember well, his sunlit face,
 So fair and hopeful, full of light divine ;
 His soul-breathed words were all the more sublime,
Because of purity and artless grace,—
Where self and sin had seemed to leave no trace.
From his glad heart, warm with devotion's glow,
Through tender lips, love had its silver flow,
And hearts, love-touched, were led to love's embrace.
In memory's halls, his youthful form I trace,
A Christly vision coming down from God ;
A few years here, in God's own ways he trod :—
And then returned to his exalted place ;
Returned, fame crowned, triumphant and complete,
Laying all honors at his dear Lord's feet.

1894.

VERNAL.

EARTH throbs with beauty !   Nature's overflow
      Of bud and blossom bursting at our feet,
   Or, o'er our heads in bending festoons meet,
   Hovering, a living crown in golden glow,—
   While bright-winged minstrels flitting to and fro,
   Busy in building all the glad day long,
   Drop from the skies a fragmentary song,
   To cheer us in our toilsome paths below.
   March frowns are past, each lengthening day a smile.
   While soft west winds nestle at quiet noon—
   Where lilacs breathing their own sweetness, swoon,
   Or fan the banks where babbling brooks beguile,
   The vernal earth, enwrapt in vernal air,
   In vernal bloom types heaven everywhere.

May 1, 1891.

HEART CULTURE.

SEARED is the soul where sin its force has wrought,
      And fruitless too, as the uncultured sod :
   Wandering away, till by the spirit taught,
      Finds the best pathways, leading back to God.
   Heart-cultivator, cultivate, till we
   Bring heart-buds, bloom, and fruit with which to
         honor Thee.

1891.

ALONE.

THE sleeping sea is sobbing,
  In tones almost a moan ;
While I walk softly near it,
  And seem to be alone.

Yet it is seeming only,
  I hear the spirit's call :
And Christ the Lord walks with me,
  The dearest Friend of all

1894.

THE MULTITUDES.

LO ! surging crowds, like the vast ocean billows,
  Press up, and onward through their sunlit ways ;
Harps taken gladly from the weeping willows,
  Are tuned to songs of heaven's exalted praise.

Press in, press in, there's room enough for all,
  Press in, press in, 'tis heaven's high festival ;
Lift high the banners, shout the " Harvest Home,"
  'Tis God's own house, the precinct of His throne.

1894.

HON. GEORGE T. COBB.

I KNEW a youth, he grew to man's estate,
　Both parents died when he was very small ;
Lonely and poor, he sought not to be great,
　But to be true and faithful, that was all.

He drove a cow to pasture every day,
　Receiving for his toil six cents a week ;
And so kept on, until some other way,
　A larger sum he could with prudence seek.

His paths, though rough, with shoeless feet he trod,
　Not long at school, he did the best he knew :
Low at the cross, he gave his heart to God,
　With God and man determined to be true.

He did not drink, or smoke, he never swore,
　High heaven smiled upon each well-laid plan ;
Each added year increased his little store,
　Before the world, he rose an honest man.

He fed the poor, God gave an hundred fold,
　　He helped the Church, and lo, his cup run o'er ;
He silver gave, God paid him back in gold,
　　He planned for God, God planned for him still more.

In Church and State, he stood divinely strong,
　　Centered in him, the pure, the good, and true ;
Lads of the land, in this my simple song,
　　His bright example I commend to you.
1892.

BEERSHEBA.

HERE thousands drink ! Then joyously along,
　　The old, the young, the reverend, and the gay,
With cheerful feet enter the place of song,
　　Devotion's shrine, where fervent spirits pray,
And drinking there the *Living Waters*, free,
They hope to drink in Heaven eternally.
1886.

TRANSLATIONS.

TRANSLATED lands, translated human hearts,
　　Translated faces by the great wide sea ;
From barren sands unfold the higher arts,
　　Childhood is gay, and age walks peacefully ;
The sky above, the earth below, are bright,
And all things glow in the translating light.
1887.

GRADUATION DAY.

𝕬𝖘𝖇𝖚𝖗𝖞 𝕻𝖆𝖗𝖐.

JOY ! We've struggled up the mountains,
 Joy ! The prospect now extends ;
Holy joy, like crystal fountains,
 With the glowing sunlight blends.

June buds burst in fragrant beauty ;
 All the air with love is sweet,
While the paths of sterner duty,
 Open to our willing feet.

Hand in hand we've toiled together,
 Heart with heart stood firm and true :
And again, before we sever,
 Friendship's pledges we renew.

Each good-bye is tinged with sadness,
 Tears are dewing love's fond eye :
Yet sometime we'll meet in gladness,
 Never more to say, Good-bye.

1888.

JOHN R. SWENEY. MUS. D.

I.

HAIL ! Joyful Sounds, immortal music, hail !
    Flood tides of bliss, with thrills of life replete,
O'er the vast earth in matchlessness prevail,
    While youth and age their lofty strains repeat,
And countless hosts, wherever man has trod,
    Touched by their spirit, gladly worship God.

II.

Music divine and song, both from above,
    Immortal twins, baptized a perfect whole !
Music and song, the dual forms of love,
    Both God-inspired to touch the human soul ;
Bright messengers of hope, white-winged with joy,
    Leading, excelsior-like, to heaven's divine employ.

1889.

" SUNLIT SONGS."

THE mists arise, the darkness flies,
   The east glows glints of gold ;
Glad song birds trill the air with life,
   The drooping flowers unfold.

There's sunlight on the mountain tops,
   There's brightness on the sea ;
There's gladness in the human soul,
   A living melody.

O sunlit songs of hope and heaven,
   Bright banners wide unfurled ;
These, flaming in the light of God,
   Illuminate the world.

O church, the night of gloom is past,
   Go forth, in high employ,—
The sorrowing of earth enthuse
   With sunlit songs of joy.

1890.

THE ALL FATHER'S LOVE.

So high, so deep, so vast,
Solemn and sacred in the soul's recesses,
Where, at low altars penitence confesses,
There, the All Father with His love caresses :
   Forgetting all the past.
Crowning the stricken heart with His forgiving smiles,
And to His own rich banquet constantly beguiles.

1894.

BISHOP PHILLIPS BROOKS.

VAST cathedral, massive, matchless, strong,
    Turret, and tower, and dome ascending high :
    Where gilded crosses flash athwart the sky,
As pealing organs lofty strains prolong ;
And aisles, and nave, and roof re-echo song,
Where candles burn, and vestments glow aflame ;
While heads are bowing at the Christly name,
Worship, like incense, rises from the throng.
But, there he stood !   Cathedral and the creed,
Turret and dome were all eclipsed in him ;
His towering thoughts made these things small indeed,
His sunlike life all churchly candles dim—
And sweeping on, an ever-widening sea,
His Christ-born love, touches infinity.

1893.

SEEDS OF LIFE.

AND we shall sow the blessed seeds of life,
    Though some may fall on hard and stony ground,—
Or by the sea, amid the swirl and strife
    Of storm-tossed waters, still, it will be found—
In the last day, some fell in mellow soil,
    Yielding an hundred-fold, O rich reward of toil.

1888.

HO. HEAVE. HO!

THE winds are cold, the seas are high,
    " Ho, heave O, Ho, heave O : "
The sea gulls as they circle nigh,
Join in the fisher's weary cry,
    " Ho, heave O, Ho, heave O,"
" The net is full," how glad the words,
Enough for men, enough for birds,
    " Ho, heave O."
Then, let us toil, for cometh so,
A full supply, through, " Ho, heave, O."
    " Ho, ho, heave O."

1888.

BIRD OF THE SEA.

BIRD of the sea, so delicate and bright,
    Born for the storm-tossed flood, and billows roar ;
Tempest or calm, thy wings of wavy light,
    Fleck the black sky, or shimmer on the shore ;
The graceful gull, peaceful amid the strife,
    Out-rides, like hope, the stormy gales of life.

1888.

ROYALTY.

WHO are those whose joyful footsteps
 Quicken with the songs they sing ?
These are they, the royal sisters,
 Noble Daughters of The King.

Cheerful hearts, the queenly household,
 Royal born to royal deeds ;
Loyal to the royal Father,
 Who supplieth all their needs.

Lo ! they come, their forms are human,
 But their faces glowing, shine ;
Every loyal act for Jesus,
 Adds another charm divine.

Hence their beauty's added splendor,
 Comes from added words of love ;
And, however small the service,
 Makes them more like those above.

Cup of water, wayside flowers,
 Gentle words and deeds, may be ;
These *Thou* givest, royal Father,
 May *Thy Daughters* give like *Thee.*

Rich or poor, or high or lowly,
 Hearts redeemed and cleansed from sin,
Plain or jeweled robes—true glory
 Is the royalty *within.*

1892.

LOYALTY!

Dedicated to the School Children of the United States of America,

Columbian Day, October 21, 1892.

I.

WITH lifted heart, and lifted hand ;
  With lifted voice and lifted brow ;
To thee, O flag, and native land,
  Our young right arms are given now.

II.

Flag of our fathers, brave and strong ;
  Flag of our mothers, fond and true :
Henceforth, each fervent prayer and song,
  Our patriot pledges shall renew.

III.

In youth or age, sickness or health,
  In shade or shine, in weal or woe ;
On land or sea, in want or wealth,
  Flag of our hearts forever glow.

IV.

Down, treason, down !   Each loyal heart
  Forever cries, Down, treason, down ;
Up, royal flag !   Each hand takes part,
  And loyalty wears honor's crown.

1892.

REV. B. M. ADAMS.

THREE score and ten ! We bid thee welcome, brother,
    Up the broad plateau of seventy years ;
The ascent grand, grander than any other,
    Hopes all sublime, eclipsing human fears ;
Here hand in hand *we stand*, one decade *both* embracing,
    While each with tear-dewed eyes life's winding paths are
        tracing.

And yet we toil ! Our toil the holiest pleasure,
    The vineyard blossoms and ripe fruits appear ;
God's love within, a still increasing measure,
    More heaven bestows with every passing year :
Until each day entranced with these divine unfoldings,
    We sink into the image of these high beholdings.

And thus I greet thee, brother of my spirit,
    Whose holy bearings have enthused my soul ;
May thou, and I, and all we love, inherit
    Crown, palm and heaven, while endless ages roll.
And from our works on earth find ever rich surprises,
    While from our glowing hearts heaven's ceaseless praise
        arises.

1894.

HEART BEATS.

BRIGHT skies above, the blue depths far below,
    The ceaseless billows, heart-beats of the sea :—
Where soft winds sigh, or tempests wail in woe,
    Eternal all, or so they seem to be ;
While generations quickly come and go,
    With briefest sighs of love, or longer wails of woe.

1887.

BEAUTIFUL SEA.

THE sea is very beautiful,
    The ever sounding sea ;
The mountains as they kiss the sky,
    In love's sublimity ;
The storm and calm are beautiful,
    The quiet and the grand ;
The storm upon the surging sea,
    The peaceful on the land.

HIGH AND DRY.

SO, human hopes lie blasted on the shore,
    So, human sorrow wails through tempests wild ;
Yet, even here, come pleadings o'er and o'er,
    Like a fond father calling for his child :
Bowed spirit, cheer, though hopes in ruin lie,
Up, God will bless, and help thee, to the sky.

1888.

REV. SAMUEL VANSANT.

I.

HIS ministry a meadow green,
  Fragrant with flowers of varied hue ;
The rain and sunshine fall between,
  The grass is jeweled with the dew ;
Through these he led the people on,
  And fed them with the finest wheat ;
Till, lured by life's immortal dawn,
  He rose, and was at Jesus' feet.

II.

The Church of God, his mountain height,
  He had in her his loved employ ;
Her summits all aflame with light,
  His heart had tidal waves of joy.
He gazed and gazed, as raptures rise,
  Old friendship grasped the hand of friend ;
Lo, tears of gladness filled his eyes
  As heaven and earth together blend.

1890.

WEDDING ANNIVERSARY.

I.

How bright the love-lit sky !
How green and fragrant love's implanted sod,
As fresh and fair as when by Adam trod,
With his sweet consort, e'er they broke with God.
How soft the love-lit eye :
How full of bliss the love-impassioned voice,
Which fills all heaven and makes the earth rejoice.

II.

Your sky is bright to-night !
All green and fragrant love's implanted sod,
Greener than when love's pathways first were trod,
For walking on, you have not broke with God ;
And love's delicious light—
A flicker first, now an electric glow,
Which gives you here this joyous overflow.

1888.

FOUR SCORE.

PISGAH summit ! Mount of vision !
    Oh what rare delights :
  Purest sunlight, sweetest song birds,
    On the four score heights.

  Four score joys—God's widening river,
    Running to the sea :
  Oh the joy of years of doing,
    Four score though they be.

1894.

SUSANNAH.

WHITE-ROBED saint, she walked before the Lord,
    She walked before the world diffusing light ;
With all things true she held such high accord,
    That all things good were her supreme delight.
Her quiet smile, illumined from above,
    Subdued, controlled, inspired, because she ruled in love.
1895.

BEAUTIFUL.

SO love is ever beautiful,
    Love, amid thorns or flowers,
All beautiful in heaven above,
    And in this world of ours :
Our God is Love — how beautiful
    He keeps, is giving, too ;
And giving, He increases, still,
    The beautiful and true.
1877.

THE KING'S DAUGHTER.

SLOW, beneath Egyptian sunlight,
    Rolled the Nile its sacred way ;
In an ark amid the rushes,
    Lo ! a sleeping infant lay.
On his cheek a tear was gleaming,
    Who would now protection bring ?
Then the Princess, child of Pharoah,
    Came, the daughter of a King.

Jewels flash, attendants gather,
    But the royal heart has sway ;
And though robed in regal splendor,
    Stoops to wipe that tear away.
Take the child, she said, and rear it,
    Teach the truth in accents mild ;
He may come to princely manhood,
    I will pay thee, take the child.

Heathen ! Yet a high example,
    Heathen, yet a woman true;
Christ's Redeemed, God's queenly daughters,
    See the path marked out for *you*.
Many a child is lone and weeping,
    Many a heart throbs with its pain ;
You, a leader too, may cherish,
    Who will pay you back again.

1891.

ADA!

I.

A sister to the Angels,
　A spirit cleansed from sin ;
The door of heaven opened,
　She joyfully passed in.

II.

The bud of earth-born beauty,
　Warmed by the light divine ;
In the first breath of heaven,
　Unfolds to the sublime.

1895.

ALL THINGS BEAUTIFUL.

THE world is very beautiful,
　The world in which we live,
Where singing birds and gushing streams,
　Their richest music give ;
Where fragrant flowers in gorgeous dyes,
　Their sweet perfumes unfold ;
And day's retiring glories, fill
　The evening sky with gold.

1877.

EULALIE!

I.

FRAGRANT and smooth be thy pathways of duty,
  Light all the burdens thy spirit may press ;
Each care be festooned with the twinings of beauty,
  Soft with affection each holy caress.

II.

Thy tears be as bright as the dews of the morning,
  Thy sorrows all soothed with breathings of love ;
Thy regretings like stars the darkness adorning,
  Thy troubles but wings to bear thee above.

III.

Home be the centre of innocent gladness,
  Heart the bright throne of the good and the true,
Rich songs of the soul removing all sadness,
  Thy spirit entrance with raptures anew.

IV.

With God over all, sublimest and truest,
  Love always—in all—to all, and adore ;
His glory thy aim, in all that thou doest,
  Then, thou shalt be His—He thine, evermore !

1890.

THE ONLY CHILD.

ONE downy nest, affection's holy centre,
  Where one lone birdling dwelt ;
Where, in His presence, who had kindly lent her,
  Fond parents often knelt.

Watching, quick glances saw her plumage changing—
  Saw soft white wings unfold :
Then, flash in light, through worlds eternal ranging,
  Where cities are of gold.

Sad songs were sung, sad songs of deep contrition,
  Over the empty nest :
Until subdued, sinking in full submission,
  Hearts found the higher rest.

Now, through the silent years, in quiet gladness,
  Parents serenely wait,
To meet her, glorified, beyond all sadness,
  At heaven's reunion gate.

1884.

PARADISE PARK.

O PARADISE Park ! In the light of thy smile,
    I have walked in the noon of my joy ;
While soft whispers of peace my spirits beguile,
    And my thoughts find their sweetest employ.

The mocking birds sing in this quiet retreat,
    And the pine trees are soughing in air ;
While the song in my soul makes rapture complete,
    As I rest from my burden of care.

Away from the bustle and hurry of time,
    Where the world and its worries control,
I rise on the wings of devotion sublime,
    Where divinity welcomes the soul.

O Paradise Park ! From thy walks I shall rise,
    To another far better than this ;
Away, far away, all unsinn'd-stained it lies,
    Where my peace finds perfection of bliss.

Thomasville, Ga., March 27, 1890.

WIDENING SEA.

HOW the sea widens as we outward sail !
    This shell, will it hold to carry us o'er?
There is fear, but faith and hope will prevail,
    The sky is all bright, and blessed the shore ;
O Father above, our trust is in Thee,
    Our Pilot divine o'er the great wide sea.

1888.

ECCE HOMO!

LAW from Sinai's summit thunders,
   Peace songs Bethlehem's plains adorn,
Lo ! the whole creation wonders,
   Christ is of a woman born.

Wave the palms, the Saviour cometh,
   Each and all his graces share :
List ! the joyful tidings runneth,
   Jesus blesses everywhere.

Sufferings come ! Garden of sorrow,
   Bloody sweat is falling down ;
The betrayal ! On the morrow,
   Cross, spikes, spear and thorny crown.

Sin in deadly insurrection,
   Rending rocks, expiring groan :
"It is finished." Resurrection
   Life sits on the victor's throne.

Hail triumphant Christ ! Forever,
   Highest praises shall arise :
Barred against us, henceforth, never,
   Gates of blessed paradise.

Wave the palms of Easter gladness,
   Wave them in the sunlit air ;
Past the days of gloom and sadness,
   Hope has blossomed everywhere.

1893

WINNING SONGS.

I.

THERE is a song which a child can sing,
    A song which is sure to win ;
Simple and sweet, its refrain will bring,
    A sigh from the heart of sin.

II.

It tells of Christ, and the Father's love,
    It tells of the heavenly rest ;—
Of the smile of God, and the home above,
    And the good forever blest.

III.

These tender songs, sung with love aglow,
    And soft with the spirit's sigh :—
Awaken thoughts of the long ago,
    And the loved ones in the sky,

IV.

So may these songs, in their winnings, win
    Great hosts from every clime ;
And winning all from the paths of sin,
    Bring the victor's song sublime.

1892.

TRUTH.

TRUTH is mighty ! Steady, forward,
    Through the vales, across the moors ;
O'er the rugged mountain summits,
    Every step success assures.

1894.

WORK.

BIND the sheaves in the bundle of life,
  Bind them ever with cords of love :
 Gather them in from the world's hot strife,
  Into the garners of heaven above :
 Gather them in, yes, gather them in,
 Gather them in from this world of sin,
 Wisest are they who the most shall win,
 Life's great work is to gather them in.

1893.

REWARD.

   All youthfulness is gay !
 Matrons and sires grow young ; the reapers sing ;
 Through all the Churches, songs of triumph ring ;—
 And all rejoice in this " Heart Harvesting."
   Glad Ocean Grove, each day,
 Hold thou to this great work, and gathering in—
 Another ransomed Soul, shall make one less in sin.

1893.

EARTH AND HEAVEN GLAD.

   Joy in the harvest field !
 O blessed work, the Summer's cheerful choice :
 Billows of wheat in the glad sun rejoice,
 Or, falling before the shouting reaper's voice :
   But, when proud spirits yield,
 And weeping, bow and ask to be forgiven,
 There's higher joy on earth, and holier bliss in heaven.

1893.

LOVE AND HOPE.

O LIGHT of love, O joy of hope,
    O bliss of God supreme ;
  Far out beyond our vision's scope,
    Extends the hallowed dream.

There is no end to holy love,
    None to God-given joy ;
  Without, within, below, above,
    They live in heaven's employ.

Such love is not a meteor's glow,
    Such hope-buds never blight ;
  The bliss of both have endless flow,
    Their day without a night.

They are not of terrestrial birth,
    But from diviner sod ;
  They bloom and fruit while on the earth,
    Because they root in God.

  1894.

SUNLIGHT, O SUNLIGHT!

SUNLIGHT ! O sunlight, there's gladness in thee,
    The darkness retires, the world is aglow :
  Song in the forests, and joy on the sea,
    There's splendor above, and splendor below,
  Hail the glad sunrise, unfollowed by night,
  Hail the glad glow of Eternity's light.

  1888.

GEORGE W. CHILDS.

HE did not covet wealth or high renown,
Nothing of earth or time, for their own sake ;
   Whatever good these give, they could not make,
For the immortal, an immortal crown ;
Or thornless paths for weary feet, or down
For throbbing temples, or sin-fever'd brain ;
But sought and found in pathways of the just
And used for God, as his own stewards must,
Bring to the soul rich blessings in their train,
Which will, when earthly things have pass'd, remain.
Such was thy course, O Childs, for thou dids't share
With others largely, God's good gifts, to thee,
Thou, His wise steward, planning noiselessly,
By whom God daily answered daily prayer.

1894.

GREETINGS.

GREETINGS to all, who these glad words receive,
     May gladness glow in every heart and eye ;
Greetings to all who in our Lord believe,
     Greetings of faith, and hope, and charity ;
To all, we wish the joy that never endeth,
Where light, and life, and love forever blendeth.

1888.

DOVES.

BENEATH the Cross, the cooing doves can rest,
     Sweetly secure, above the surging sea :
Here, here alone, can human hearts be blest,
     And find their refuge, Holy Christ, in Thee.
Saviour divine, here let my soul abide,
And, like the doves, may we sit side by side.

1889.

GOD EVER.

GOD was the first, and He should ever be
     First, last, and always in the human heart :
Eternal One, my spirit looks to Thee.
     In all my ways take Thou the leading part,
So let my song be while the earth is trod, —
All through my life, " *In the beginning God.*"

1889.

RESCUE.

ON, on to the rescue, a life is in peril,
     On, on hardy seaman, the honest and true,
On, on, O ye Christians, a soul is in danger,
     And largely the rescue is resting on you.
On, onward, O seaman, On, onward, O saint,
     Let faith never falter, nor firmness grow faint.

1889.

FAITH.

THROUGH adverse winds and tides,
  Tempest, and starless night,
 Our bark triumphant rides,
  Faith-borne, into the light.

1889.

COMBINATION.

SUN, earth and air, combining with the dew,
 Unfold the seeds, then stem, and bud, and bloom,—
Exquisite tints, pink, violet, and blue,
 Smile in the light, and breathe their rich perfume.
So, by the sea, in love's divine employ,
 Hearts blossom out, in God's enduring joy.

1890.

ROSE TINTED PROPHECY.

THE morning breaks ! Rose-tinted prophecy—
 As when a child is born, and joy-bells ring ;
Health-breathing breezes, rollicking and free,
 Like gulls, glide o'er the waves. The billows sing.
The danger passed. Night's sable banners furled,
 The rising sun, with splendor floods the world.

1890.

FOREST TEMPLE.

THE grand old forest, nature's temple vast,
 White tents, rude seats and rustic pulpit high :
Great sermons ! night ! pine blaze weird shadows cast,
 And songs, and prayers and praise ascend the sky :
While souls, new-born, rejoice e'er rise of sun,
 And hearts aflame with love, rejoice, God's work is done.

1890.

CLARENCE.

CHILDHOOD and youth, like merry-footed May
   Trip o'er the mead, only a narrow span ;
The flowers unfold, ascends God's golden day,
   New life evolves, behold the blushing man !
The blushing man with inspiration rife,
On the bright threshold of a nobler life.

I greet thee, Clarence, on this high attain,
   A rise above all childhood, broad and strong ;
Keep true and steady, thou shalt rise again,
   For all true life, however short or long,
Is made of rises, till the great arise,
By which, with help divine, we reach the skies.

A child of Avon and of Ocean Grove ;
   May the All Father hold thee in His hand,
And may thy spirit touched by His sweet love
   Always respond to each divine command ;
So all along, thy soul, in God complete,
Thy last great rise may be to His dear feet.

1892.

BEAUTY.

Beauty above, below,
And all around, on land, the sea, and sky :
Where sunshine sleeps, or where the storms sweep by,
Through winding vales, where scented lilies lie,
   And fragrant breezes blow :
Until as lakes, reflect the heaven above,
Show us while here on earth, the higher heaven of love.

1892.

EDNA.

GO, baby girl, sweet rosebud, Edna, go ;
  Bud of our hearts go, blossom in the skies ;
Our souls are touched, for we have loved thee so,
  And tears of sadness fall from sorrow's eyes ;—
But, grief finds solace in God's holy love,
She shall be ours again, in bowers above.

1892.

TRIUMPH.

ON bloody battle field,
    Lay broken sword and shield,
Cutlas and sabre, with the shattered lance,
  Horses, whose daring flight,
  Rushed to the fiercest fight,
While pealing trumpets sounded the advance.

    There, too, lay 'neath the sun,
    A man, whose work was done,
A dying soldier, on his gory bed ;
    Gladness was in his eye,
    " Triumph " was his cry,
Peace filled his heart and glory crowned his head.

1894.

PRAISE IN SONG.

I.

From the beginning praise
Has best expressed itself in holy song;
By the lone heart or the exultant throng;
So childhood, youth, and hoary age prolong
Gladness in jubal lays.
On mountain heights, or by the rolling sea,
Let every heart break forth in hallowed melody.

II.

Here, heaven and earth unite—
Song fell from heaven when Christ the Lord was born,
Song cheers the heart when earth is all forlorn:
Then, sing at night, and in the early morn;
Sing in supreme delight:
Sing praise to God; go, praise Him, and adore,
Till all shall meet above, then praise forevermore.

1893.

HARVEST HOME.

Forever there,
On the far heights with all the ransomed host,
From every land, or calm or stormy coast,
Redemption's themes forever uppermost;
While everywhere
High Jubal songs to every tongue are given,
The Harvest Home, true rest, and earth
Exchanged for heaven.

1894.

COL. GEORGE W. BAIN.

GOD bless our noble orator,
  Kentucky's honored son,
His flights are like the eagle's,
  Which rise towards the sun.
We gaze upon his pictures,
  His thoughts each spirit cheers,
His tender utterances inspire,
  And start, or dry our tears.

His fame glows on the mountains,
  It flashes through the vales ;
It breathes through summer zephyrs,
  It rushes on the gales.
We hear it in the evening,
  A soft and sweet refrain,
And lo ! the morning's dewy light
  Flashes, GEORGE W. BAIN !

1893.

EPWORTH LEAGUE.

RISE, Epworth's sons and daughters,
    Strive for the good and true ;
The field is vast, and widely
    Each day unfolds to you :—
Bring back your wayward brothers,
    With erring sisters weep ;
And bridge, with Scripture promises,
    Sin's fearful chasms deep.

Combine to help the helpless,
    Sow light where darkness reigns ;
In hearts all crushed with sorrow,
    Scatter love's golden grains ;
Wait not for great occasions,
    For every day and hour,
Kind words a thorn extracting,
    Will substitute a flower.

Pray much ! Be earnest hearted,
    And Christ-like in your speech—
Your words, then, Spirit guided,
    Remotest lands may reach ;
Do, and the Lord will bless you ;
    Be, and find heaven below ;
Then every step ascending,
    Will brighten as you go.

1894.

GIFTS.

ARBUTUS smiles, the first faint smile of spring,
　　After the frozen frown of wintry wrath—
Awakening gladness, and the blue birds sing
　　Among the breaking buds in April's path.

The pitcher plant, awaiting high commands,
　　Ready to serve with dignity apace ;
Bearing the wine of God in both her hands,
　　Succors the modest flowers with modest grace.

My warmest thanks for both these fragrant gifts,
　　Sun-tinted bloom in nature's pitchers, rare ;
As from the heart, each flower some sorrow lifts,
　　So may you find it always, everywhere.

Easter Week, 1890.

AIR.

BLESSED, God-given air,
　　Existing everywhere ;
In valleys low, or on the mountain path ;
　　In tempests or in calm,
　　Singing a holy psalm,
When zephyrs sigh, or wails the wintry wrath.

　　And yet they both retire,
　　And both worn out, expire,
As dies the rose wreath at the touch of night ;
　　The struggle and the strife
　　Evolve in peaceful life,
As when the darkness kisses morning's light.

1893.

THE TRUE CHURCH.

I.

THE Church of God is not alone
    The brick, and stone, foundation, roof ;
But hearts, where God erects his throne,
    And spirit life makes warp and woof :
Not simply where high organs peal,
    Or gathers the uncounted host,
But where the fervent spirits kneel,
    And worship in the Holy Ghost.

II.

Nor this alone ! But every heart,
    A glowing flame, devoted, true ;
Men, women, children, taking part,
    And doing what they find to do ;
All thus engaged in toil divine,
    God sought, received, obeyed, adored—
The soul renewed, becomes sublime,
    And earth is paradise restored.

III.

The circuit preacher ! Broad brimmed hat,
    Clothing of honest homespun made ;
His long great coat and white cravat
    Are neat without artistic aid.
His saddle-bags ! His faithful grey !
    His Bible, hymn book, discipline ;
And reading Wesley every day,
    Equipped and strong, he goes to win.

1889

UP FROM THE BEACH.

UP from the beach, joy-robed, with sunlit faces,
 Through green-leaved groves, go to the House of God ;
 High audience there, go up with love's quick paces,
  Where sainted feet delightedly have trod.
 Heart-songs, soul-prayers, here reach the ear on high,
 And love, which never fails, gives back love's quick reply.
1892.

DEVOTION.

UP to the House of God fond hearts repair,
 Souls all aglow with pure devotion's fires :—
 Hold high communion through each fervent prayer,
  Where human songs blend with celestial choirs :
 Sires, matrons, children, pressing towards the skies,
 Each step God-guided, a divine arise.
1892.

SMALL BEGINNINGS.

I.

A flickering ray, at first so small,
　　None seemed to know from whence it came ;
Yet, destined to o'ershadow all,
　　And sweep, an all consuming flame ;
One silent man, almost unknown,
　　With joyful heart, yet weeping eyes,
Came through the southern pines alone,
　　And lit the lamp that flushed the skies.

II.

And so, the fire began to burn,
　　And so the light began to spread ;
Men from their sins began to turn,
　　And sorrow's heart was comforted.
The years roll on, and truth divine,
　　Immortal seeds, take root beneath ;
And towering, they rise sublime,
　　Beyond the touch of frost and death.

III.

Ring, ring the bells ! the church complete,
　　The walls are plain, the pulpit high ;
Yet saints unite for sin's defeat,
　　And all the powers of hell defy.
To outward sight no charms appear,
　　Yet human hearts with joy o'erflow ;
The unplaned planks, though rough, are dear,
　　And all within has glory's glow.

1889.

MAY.

THROUGH the chime of vesper bells,
  Softest, sweetest music swells ;
Sweetest tones through all the air,
Throbbing sweetness everywhere.

Music's daughter, full of love,
Goes to sing her songs above ;
 . But the evening's silken wings,
Bringeth back heart welcomings.

In her old, yet new employ,
Heaven overflows with joy ;
We are comforted below
With the blessed overflow.

Hearts of sorrow thus are soothed,
Ways of roughness kindly smoothed.
O, the blessedness ! when we
Join her songs eternally.

1895.

SERMONS IN SONG.

I.

FAR out o'er the wild Red Sea,
   The tones of triumph rang ;
As Miriam told of victory,
   In the high notes she sang.

II.

And all the people joined the song—
   Sires, matrons, maidens, sing ;
For right had triumphed over wrong,
   The Lord himself was King.

III.

But lo ! amid Judean hills,
   Still other songs are heard ;
Love songs which every nation fills,
   And human hearts are stirred.

IV.

Soft songs of peace, sweet songs of love,
   To man, by angels given ;
High songs of joy, dropped from above,
   And leading back to heaven.

V.

Go, sing these ever blessed songs,
   Sermons in songs proclaim ;
Salvation to the Lord belongs,
   O blessed be His Name!

1894

GLADNESS.

I.

RING, ring the bells, there's joy above,
  Ring, ring the bells, there's joy below !
The voice of God, immortal love,
  Is heard, and hearts are all aglow.
Down from my mountain's lofty height,
  I see the church of God arise—
While holy men, filled with delight,
  Look on its walls in glad surprise.

II.

So came the Church ! so preachers came,
  Great men of God, sedate, serene ;
Their souls inspired, a furnace flame,
  And sent of God, they stood between
The living and the dead.   When lo !
  Sin is dethroned, the law maintained,
Sinai and Calvary are aglow,
  And Christ for all, to all proclaimed.

III.

The human heart a wreck complete,
  But Christ a Saviour, all divine ;
In Him, sin's empire finds defeat,
  And over all, men rise sublime.
Expelled from paradise by sin,
  We rise from sin's terrific fall ;
By Christ again we enter in,
  And loss is gain, when Christ is all.

1889.

MINISTERIAL CLASS REUNION OF 1844.

THE five decades are past ! we have not sought
  Through the long conflict for earth's poor renown ;
But armed of God, the fight of faith have fought,
  And have this day secured the golden crown ;—
The golden crown, not of eternal life,
  But that which marks the close of fifty years of strife.

God-given years ! How blessed all their days ;
  Their toil sweet rest, defeats their triumphs won ;
If paths were rough, they led to smoother ways :
  O'er darkest nights soon rose a brighter sun ;
And savage seas bowed down to holy calms.
  While discord tuned the lyre to love's delicious psalms.

Comrades have fallen ! Noble men of might;
  Fallen ? Nay, nay, risen to summits high ;
Beyond the sun, beyond the stars of light,
  To zones of brightness which all thoughts defy,
White-robed, love-crowned, eternal victors there,
  Amazement all ! with God, unending bliss to share.

We tarry yet ! Life's work still incomplete !
  Help us to finish, wisely, Lord for Thee :
The little done, we lay at Thy dear feet,
  Wishing it had been wrought more perfectly.
When all is through, Father, for us provide
  Sweet rest with Thee, and them, and all the glorified.

1894.

PLUME OF THE BILLOW.

THE billow's plume is the wind-kissed wave,
  Where it crests the frosted silver spray ;
 Like the helmets' toss of warriors brave,
    Marching in strength on the victors' way.
1894.

TELEGRAPH.

SPACE is conquered, knowledge flies,
  Lightning winged through all the skies ;
 But our prayers ascend to God,
 Ways by swifter angels trod.

1894.

HEART FRUIT.

FRUIT by the sea ! Heart Fruit ! Love, joy, and peace,
  The spirit's gifts ! Redemption's rich supplies ;
 These, all expanding, God's divine increase,
   Bring ripening tints, soul blushes from the skies ;
 While Ocean Grove, through all, sends forth its song,
  Greeting each one, through Him, to whom we all belong.
1892.

E

"BITTER SWEET."

"THERE is nothing so bad, that it might not be worse."
     Thus runs the old proverb, and it mainly is true ;
Yet life's ills could combine for an unheard of curse,
    All the more to be dreaded because something new.

Yet there's throbbings of hope in the heart of despair,
    There are star glints of joy in the night's deepest gloom ;
There are tender lute tones through the tempest tossed air.
    And germs of new life in the mould of the tomb.

There is sorrow in love, and there's gladness in grief,
    Sweet peace in the tumult which no foes can prevent ;
The heart bending lowest finds surest relief,
    And the self-renounced will the divinest content.

Then be steady and true, for our Father is good,
    If the eagle claims mountains, the mole has his hill ;
The place He assigns us, let it be understood,
    Is our place, and true peace is accepting His will.

1894.

TENDERNESS.

HOW warm thy heart, how soft thine eye.
    Thy words distill like honey dew ;
    Love's tender song brings love's reply,
      And love's old words are always new !

1889.

GULIELMA!

JOY comes to thee, O bridegroom,
   Joy in this tender way ;
Through graceful art, of hand and heart,
    Of Gulielma !

Accept it as from heaven,
   On this appointed day ;
For gloom of night, is touched with light,
    By Gulielma !

1892.

THE BUTTERFLY.

NO matter where, no matter when,
   By rolling sea, on mountains high,
'Mid solitudes, or throngs of men,
   With well-trained heart and skillful eye ;
We, if we never cease to try,
   On mountain top, or by the sea,
Shall, like the busy butterfly,
   Find good that is, or yet to be.

1892.

LOVE AND PRAISE.

THE love of God, all human love transcending,
    Fondest and purest, sweetest and the best ;
Without beginning it shall have no ending,
    Proceeding from, and leading to, the blest.
Royal-enrobed in all enduring splendor,
Grieved by neglect, yet in forgiveness tender.

Bound ransomed hearts ! High joy excludes the sadness,
    All tongues enthused, extol eternal love ;
Enwreathed with smiles comes tripping sunlit gladness,
    Each blessed note an echo from above,
While songs of love and praise, mingling together,
Increase the bliss of heaven, always, forever !
1894.

THE CROSS.

THE bloody Cross precedes the rocky tomb,
    The rocky tomb, the resurrection morn ;
The golden light follows the midnight gloom,
    The smiles of God, the fiercest earthly scorn ;
The Lord Christ suffered all His pathways, through,
Courage, O Saint, He triumphed, so shall you.
1887.

LILLIAN.

THE laurels are wet on the mountains,
　　The forests are jewelled with rain ;
Yet brightness unfolds in the valleys
　　Where love sings her holy refrain.
O Lillian, fair as the snowflake,
　　But warm as the kiss of the sun;
The fond and the fervent are mated,
　　The mated and married are one.

Though the clouds may darken the heavens,
　　Love lightens the sky of the soul ;
Rich rainbows of hope in their splendor,
　　With gladness are spanning the whole.
O love, thou art strong in the sunlight,
　　But stronger when darkness shall frown ;
New sorrows give birth to new triumphs,
　　New griefs add new gems to thy crown.

June, 1889.

ELIZABETH.

I.

Another mile-stone gained !
Another summit reached, skyward ascent ;
Extending views, a brighter firmament ;
Diviner joys, a holier content,—
     A broader life attained ;—
Low at the feet of Him, highest of all,
This birthday blessedness, the soul's fond festival.

II.

     Touched with the light of love,
Earth's darkest scenes grow bright, its wild waves still,
Its deepest griefs heaven's holy laws fulfill ;
And sweetest peace, no more a rippling rill,
     But, flowing from above,
Widens to rivers, oceans, shoreless, deep,
Where angel zephyrs, soft, in mellow murmurs sweep.

III.

So may this birthday here,
'Mid sunny South-lands, blossomings and song,
Where fruits abound, and tides of life are strong,
Be a bright pledge that life for thee is long,—
  And full of holy cheer :
Thy sunny home, husband, and children, friends,
Type to thy tranquil soul, the life that never ends.
Somerville, S. C., 1895.

LILIES AROUND THE CROSS.

I.

NEVER mind the deepest sorrow,
  Never mind the greatest loss ;
In the light of glad to-morrow,
  Lilies will entwine the cross.

II.

If the way is rough and thorny
  Promises are as the moss :
Burdens heavy, sky all stormy,
  Lilies still entwine the cross.
Easter Eve, 1890.

OUR QUEEN.

I.

Sitting a queenly queen,
Amid the '' Daughters of the King of Kings,''
There, as we rise upon devotion's wings,
Thy quiet smile the sweetest gladness brings ;
　　　In sorrow's depths, serene ;
Thy voice, subdued, with tenderness replete,
Has held us, loving captives, at thy feet.

II.

What shall we render thee,
Oh, gentle lady, who has loved us so ?
Whose glowing heart has set us all aglow
In our own grief, to soothe some other's woe,
　　　With fondest fervency ;
To thee, Our Queen, our truest love we give,
And as King's Daughters, pledge ourselves to live.

III.

Our aching bosoms swell !
A shadow crosses all our sunlit skies,
Our spirits droop, while tears bedew our eyes,
Each burdened heart its silent sorrow sighs ;
　　　One sweet, but sad farewell ;
Yet to us all, hope trills her rich refrain,
Here, or beyond, the good shall meet again.

1889.

PEARL.

HER face full of sunshine, no clouds can destroy,
   Her heart full of love, her eyes bright with joy ;
In deeds full of goodness her hands find employ.

Now, what do you think ?   Why, on Christmas, you see,
Right straight, through the post, came a picture to me,
And the folks all exclaimed, " *Why, who can it be?* "

I'll tell you at once : Why, the dear little girl,
With the long flowing hair, inclining to curl,
And bright sunny face, is just, Little Pearl.

She's come to stay with us, you see, all the while,
The long weary hours of our life to beguile,
And cheer up our home with the light of her smile.

So, now, when folks ask, " Whose is this little girl,
With the long flowing hair, inclining to curl ? "
We say, " Don't you know ? It's our *own* Little Pearl."

1887.

NEARING THE HARBOR.

I.

There's light across the sea !
The tempest's moans have sunk into a sigh,
The billows sleep, there's brightness in the sky,
Gladness is beaming in affection's eye,
      Love sings her lullaby,
And hope at four score, patiently and calm
Is singing here, the victor's endless psalm.

II.

Courage ; O, saint !
The tempests in thy sky are overpast,
The weary sea-leagues are receding fast :
Land ! land ahead ! God's own bright land at last.
      The heart, no longer faint,—
Inspired, like storm-tossed men on reaching shore,
Who leap to land, and live forevermore.

III.

O, cheer thee, cherished friend !
The toils of four score years are fully done,
And, like the splendor of the setting sun,
Earth's rest and heaven's are blending into one,
      Where human labors end,
And break, like billows of a sunlit sea,
In blessed bliss of God—eternally.

1889.

EIGHTY-SEVEN.

I.

EIGHTY-SEVEN ! Lengthening shadows
    Show the close of day ;
  Eighty-seven, nearing heaven,
    Shadows melt away.
  Eighty-seven ! oh, the journey,
    Weariness and care ;
  But, to ease us, Holy Jesus
    Guides through gloom and glare.

II.

  Eighty-seven ! Ever changing,
    Sea, and human breast ;
  Glint and glimmer, sigh and shimmer,
    Tempest roar and rest.
  Eighty-seven ; through the dangers,
    Every pathway trod,
  High or lowly, leaning wholly,
    Enoch-like, on God.

III.

  Eighty-seven ! Lengthening shadows
    Show the close of day ;
  Eighty-seven, nearing heaven,
    Shadows melt away.
  Shadows pass, the substance lingers,
    Light and love and joy,
  Exit sadness, enter gladness,
    Oh, the grand employ!

1886.

DUAL ANNIVERSARY.

GLAD day of birth, glad golden wedding day !
   Fond memory revels in supreme delight ;
The morning glad, the noon, and glad the night,
And love enthroned, chants her exalted lay.
Love's diamonds flash in their own native way,
Love's tones rebound, love's sunlit billows roll,
While tides of bliss go throbbing through the soul,
And love, white-robed, holds the imperial sway.
Love's hearthstones glow with sweet affection's fire,
Love's pathways bloom with hope's enchanting hues,
Love's flowers expand, nourished by love's fresh dews,
Till in the round of life, all these expire,—
Then love, expectant, sees the skies unfold,
And, smiling, waits God's wedding day of gold.

1889.

IN ALL WEATHER.

I HEAR the murmur of the crystal springs,
   Whose pulses throb, on through the summer's heat ;
And through the winter's wail, sweet whisperings—
   As if, mid tempests and the burnished sleet,
Their joys were highest, while their silver flow,
Sun-tipped, dash through the mead enwrapt in virgin
     snow.

1895.

RHODA.

THE sun comes in the morning,
   Bidding the darkness flee ;
His beams revive the flowers,
   And brighten all the sea.

The dews fall in the evening,
   Softly and silently,
Giving to every flower
   A pearl of brilliancy.

Both sun and dew are givers,
   With, or without display ;
Their joy is in diffusing,
   Each in their quiet way.

So in life's golden morning,
   Like sunshine and the dew ;
Our Rhoda's gifts of gladness
   Are beautiful and true.

1895.

OUR PASTOR.

I.

JOY to our pastor !   Joy !
    Joy to his queenly wife !
Twenty-five years—inwrought with fears—
        Have had through all the strife,
        Such blessed high employ,
That through each storm appears
Rainbows, new born, from thickly falling tears.

II.

    Joy ! Mountain summits high,
        Through passes rough and steep,
Are reached at last, the roughest passed ;
        All others faith can leap ;
        So, pressing towards the sky,
Though clouds may shadows cast,
Visions break through, of glowing grandeur vast.

III.

    " Joy ! " older people say ;
        " Joy ! " cries the ardent youth ;
The joy bells ring, the children sing,
        A blessed song, forsooth ;
        Joy blossoms all the way,
        Joy in all sorrowing,—
Then boundless joy through heaven's eternal spring.

1890.

DEATH'S TRIUMPH.

MOTHER'S kiss is life's holy dew,
　　And the young wife's hope is bright,
While the lisping loves of childhood true,
　　Fill home's sweet bowers with light.

But Death comes in to darken the skies,
　　And to blast the June buds through ;
" What to me," he says, " are love-lit eyes,
　　Or what are the fond hearts true?"

I can dash the cup from lips of bliss,
　　Can say to each heart be still :
Can put out the light from worlds like this,
　　I can, I have, and I will!

And then, when the morning light broke in,
　　The tent in its beauty lay :
But he who had slept there, free from sin,
　　Awoke in the realms of day.

Then loved ones sit by the fallen tent,
　　With their hearts still beating true :
They say, " The tenant was only lent,
　　And the Lord has claimed His due."

Oh, the heart of love is a sacred boon,
　　Earth's brightest jewel given :
Though the human side expires so soon,
　　The Christly lives in heaven.

1887.

A MAIDEN.

IN the valley, lone and lowly ;
   Walked a maiden fair ;
Twining fondly fragrant blossoms,
   In her golden hair.

On the hill tops, through the meadows,
   By the brooklet's side ;
Softly, like the silvery waters,
   She, a maiden, sighed.

Eyes, were like the stars above her,
   Face, a vision bright :
And her coming brought the gladness,
   As the sun brings light.

Bright her eyes with pure affection,
   Others bright, replied ;
Love was born in two fond bosoms,
   Two fond lovers sighed.

Is there in this realm of sorrow
   Any sweeter bliss :
In the cup of human gladness,
   Joy so full as this ?

All the sky above is brighter,
   All aglow the vale ;
As we sing in holy measure,
   Love's delicious tale.

1884.

BERTHA.

LITTLE ferns and mosses,
  Wear their dewy crowns ;
Though they may have crosses,
  Never show their frowns.

So our bonny lasses,
  By the lakes or sea ;
Beautiful as sunlight,
  Smile as cheerfully.

Multitudes of grasses,
  Springing from the sod ;
Lift their glowing dewdrops,
  Each reflecting God.

So, of all the pleasures
  In the paths of youth ;
Bertha finds her sweetest
  In the words of Truth.

1895.

VICTORIA.

Fifty Years a Queen.

VICTORIA !   A golden reign,
    Of fifty tried and trusted years;
The Empress of a wide domain,
    A Koh-i-noor amid thy peers.

Around the globe thy power is felt,
    On every sea thy banners glow;
Thy highest fame when thou hast knelt,
    To Him from whom true honors flow.

Thy throne, more than a golden throne,
    Thy crown, illustrious as the light,
Thy sceptre, swayed for truth alone,
    A jewelled ensign of the right.

Back fifty years !   A maiden fair,
    A royal maiden, pure and good:
But nobler now, though marked with care,
    In all thy royal motherhood.

A woman's reign !   Yet wise and true,
    A woman's reign !   Revile it not;
A woman's reign !   The past review,
    A woman's reign ! without a blot.

Hail woman !   Queen of home and heart,
    Thy sceptre wave o'er sea and sod,
Thy rule is love's divinest art,
    Thy reign, next to the reign of God.

June 15, 1887.

THE BISHOP'S DAUGHTER.

SWEET Mays will blossom into Junes—Sweet Junes,
    Delicious all day long ;
Sweet notes will marshal into tunes—sweet tunes,
    In one harmonious song.

The mountain springs widen to streams—sweet streams,
    Then broaden into bays ;
And nights are lighted up with dreams—sweet dreams,
    Then lost in golden days.

The valleys bright wear beauty's smile—sweet smile,
    Where gentle waters flow ;
Childhood and youth here wait awhile—sweet while,
    Till buds to blossoms grow.

And so our *May* stepped into June—sweet June,
    In such a royal way ;
May—June, meet soon, echo replies—*sweet soon*,
    On graduation day.

From beauty's vale, ascending slopes—sweet slopes,
    With rainbows arched above ;
The glowing heart rebounds with hopes—sweet hopes,
    And life is crowned with love.

Summer unfolds, the household pet—sweet pet,
    Still ours, our own, alway ;
And yet, things change, and *yet*, and YET—sweet YET,
    Our JUNE, is *now* in MAY.

1888.

JESUS.

JESUS! Human infant, weeping.
  On His mother's lowly knee ;
Jesus, weary, pillowed, sleeping,
  As He sails o'er Galilee.

Jesus! Saviour, balm for sadness,
  Hope for all, a joyful sound ;
Let the tidings, full of gladness,
  Roll the sin-girt earth around.

Jesus, Star! shines out in splendor;
  Jesus, Sun, brings in the day ;
Jesus, voicing accents tender,
  Bids me come to Him, The Way.

Jesus, Master! kindly knocking,
  At the door of every heart ;
Gladly now, my soul unlocking,
  Welcomes Thee to every part.

Jesus! Friend of all the lowly,
  Shepherd, Prophet, Priest, and King ;
O the joy of being holy,
  O what rapture as I sing !

Jesus! Let my soul adore Thee,
  Cleansed by Thee from every sin ;
Thus renewed, bow down before Thee,
  Reach the gates and enter in.

1891.

HATTIE.

I.

SHE came from the skies like a snow-white bird,
  Perching a while on love's bosom for rest ;
Her cherub tones all fond affections stirred,
  And fond affection warmed her downy nest.

II.

A while she sung, so tenderly and sweet,
  Cheerful at dawn, and dreamily at night ;
While through her rhythmic carolings complete,
  Her wings were pluming for another flight.

III.

Away, away, to higher song-lands free,
  Earth's Eden left, for frostless gardens rare,
And fresh young life unfolding endlessly,
  The bliss of blisses finds perfection there.

1895.

HEAVEN.

OUT and away, somewhere, it will be found,
  The Central Throne, the Palace of the King,
Where God Himself his own is welcoming,
And white-robed saints eternally are crowned—
Where all celestial ecstacies abound.
The bliss of bloom, beneath the cloudless skies,
Like love, unfolds to love's bewildered eyes,
And love's soft song melts in delicious sound.
When shall I reach that high and holy clime?
My friends go up in chariots of light,
While I must wait for all their bliss sublime.
Hush! Taught of God, I rise to new delight;
And, as the lake reflects the skies above,
Find heaven abides, e'en here, in the pure heart
  of love.

1888.

NOBLER BIRTH.

CLINGING to the things of earth,
  Grant us each a nobler birth:
Ours be not the sparrow's flight,
But the eagle's, lost in light;
Wings of faith, O help us rise,
To the paths of paradise.

THE SAINTS OF GOD.

THE saints of God are marching on,
   In robes of spotless white ;
Their faces glow like morning's dawn,
   Their paths, the paths of light.

Their steps are true, their hearts beat high,
   Their songs, the songs of joy ;
There's gladness in each beaming eye,
   And heaven in their employ.

Crowns sit upon each polished brow,
   Bright crowns of living light ;
They wave the palms of victors now,
   Though passing through the fight.

Exultant march ! exultant reign !
   There's conquest in their tread ;
The foes of inward peace are slain,
   And Satan's hosts have fled.

Their banners float upon the breeze,
   The world looks in surprise,
And asks in wonder, " Who are these ? "
   " MINE, MINE ! " the Lord replies.

Bright banner'd host, your leader God,
   Once small but now so vast,
March in the light, pure thro' the blood,
   And enter heaven at last !

1889.

ABSOLUTENESS.

I.

The Lord our Holy God,
He liveth, loveth, reigneth,
Always, all things sustaineth ;
He ever so remaineth,
Creation heeds His nod : —
If man is reckless, he must understand,
That all things bend or break, at God's supreme command.

II.

Earth does not wish it so !
Man fain would be dogmatic,
But, God's ways are emphatic,
And pure love, autocratic,
Consulteth none, to know : —
Wisdom, love-swayed, is masterful for good,
And terror's reign bows down before God's Fatherhood.

1894.

ALL AT WORK.

THIS is God's way, and every heart,
A glowing flame, devoted, true ;
Men, women, children taking part,
And doing what they find to do :
All thus engaged in toil divine,
God sought, received, obeyed, adored—
The soul renewed, becomes sublime,
And earth is paradise restored.

1890.

MARY.

THE paths she walked were bright with God's sweet
     smile,
    The paths of holy duty ;
Thorny sometimes, but blossoming the while,
    Into divinest beauty.

With spirit meek and mild, she walked in white,
    Rainbows of hope above her ;
Patient and cheerful, fond home's purest light,
    And she home's fondest lover.

Parental hearts basked in her love-lit eyes,
    To them, full orbs of splendor ;
Her voice, like music from the far-off skies,
    Such as none others render.

Gone home ! The sweet beyond.   Henceforth to be
    Christ's bride, whose love had sought her :
    Bride-groom divine !   Bereft, but lovingly,
1894.   We yield our only daughter.

ADALINE.

A BURSTING bud nestled amid the bowers,
 Brightest and best, in all the garden fair ;
With tinted lips it kissed its sister flowers,
 And bathed its brow with morning's dewy air.

The gardener passed along the blooming border,
 And found it in its blushing beauty dressed ;
Then to the palace by a royal order,
 Bore the rich bloom to grace the royal breast.

Then, all the opening buds and blossoms tender,
 Envied their fair young sister, borne away ;
Thence to unfold amid the palace splendor,
 While they were left to wither and decay.

And, so your Adaline, in home's sweet bowers,
 Op'ed in her tenderness with smiles of love ;
The Gardener sought the best among the flowers,
 And claimed your bud for palace halls above.

Then do not crave her back. Forever rising,
 Though to our sight she sleeps beneath the sod ;
Soon light will break, and then, with joy surprising,
 You shall behold her blooming still with God.

We will be patient ! That which seems all sadness
 Has better meanings than we often give ;
From deepest sorrows rise the highest gladness :
 And so in death, we just begin to live.

1886.

THE SUMMIT SPRING.

BY mountain roadside, where the forest ends,
   Beneath the stern old rocks, with lichens gray ;
 Where the wild grape-vines in their graceful trends,
   From forest shades creep to the light of day ;
 Where daisies blossom, and the crickets trill,
 God brews the pure fresh water by his own sweet will.

1895.

PURITY.

NO stiffling stench from Nature's vats arise,
   No sickening fumes disgust the artless child ;
 But pure as dew-drops from the bending skies,
   God's nectar comes as dew-drops undefiled ;
 We bless the day when water first was made,
 For by this grand old beverage have our nerves been
    stayed.

1895.

RURAL.

AROUND are hills and mountains forest crowned,
   And silver lakes in emerald frames are set ;
 Here Indian camps in the stone age were found,
   And war's rude implements are gathered yet ;
 But, savagery subdued, mountains and dells
 Are startled nevermore by the wild Indians' yells.

1895.

THE ROBIN'S BATH.

HOW glad the mission of the sun-lit tides,
   Where robins bathe, and bluebirds dip their wings ;
 The autumn leaf in silent beauty glides,
   Here nestling birds learn their first carollings ;
 Refreshed the kine, the rootlets drink their fill,
 And sparkling waters flow to help the distant mill.

1895.

UPWARD.

SON of God! I look to Thee,
With compassion look on me;
Lift me by Thy smiles of love,
To the better things above;
Rule my heart, my will control,
Grant the peace which calms the soul.

When I'm wrong, O set me right,
Lift from darkness into light;
Out of winter, cold and grey,
Waft me into summer's day;
From the desert wastes of sin,—
To Thy garden take me in.

1890.

CIVILIZATION.

THE stone age gone, the iron come at last,
The silver and the golden periods, here;
The roughest rocks drop into order fast,
Unsightly forms in beauty's garb appear;
The fragrant rose-tree, and the feathery larch,
Mansion and music join the civilizing march.

1895.

PERPETUITY.

STILL the bright waters flow, the same old spring,
Soft, clear and cool, of imperfections shorn;
New ages come, but no improvements bring,
As perfect now as when it first was born,
And centuries on will be, down to the end,
For who, in this world, can perfection mend?

1895.

JENNIE AND FLOSSIE.

WE are sisters, tender sisters,
 Bound by silken cords of love ;
Held by fetters, golden fetters,
 All whose links were forged above.

We are sisters ! Happy sisters,
 Sweetly held by sacred ties.
May they hold you, ever hold you,
 Here on earth, and to the skies.

1895.

JOY.

THEN ring the bells, the soft, sweet bells ;
 Old times go out, all things are new ;
The anthem swells, ring, ring the bells—
 Ring of the all things good and true.
O ring the bells, triumphant bells ;
 Let ransomed hosts high tributes bring.
The Church of God her anthem swells,
 Let heaven and earth the joy bells ring !

1889

CROWN THE YEARS.

CROWN the five and twenty years,
  Years of smiles and years of tears ;
  Years of toil which God has blest,
  Years of weariness and rest :
  Years of sunshine more than sadness,
  Crown the silver years with gladness.

1894.

CROWNS FOR ALL.

CROWNS, crowns ! What shall we crown ? a high
    endeavor ?
  A noble stride in the straight lines of light ?
Lord, there's a crown for all who seek Thy favor,
  And with a single eye strive for the right.
These crowns will fit the highest and the lowly,
  The royal king, the beggar or the slave ;
Crowns none can wear unless the heart is holy,
  And to be holy, Christ the Lord must save.
Lord, crown this Seaside Service, and its untold story,
  And if it please Thee, us, with all Thy widening glory.

1894.

ANGELS CROWN THEM.

    Angels of God descend !
Spirit illume, unveil the Great White Throne :
All that the soul may see to us be shown,
And all the knowable to us make known ;
    Divine refinements, blend
With things below. Ethereal realms unfold,
And silver crowns precede the richer crowns
    of gold.

1894.

IDA.

Thy home was love's retreat !
Affection's throne, with God's imparted grace ;
A downy nest, where love had fond embrace,
Where smiles enwreathed each gentle love-lit face,
　　Where love's soft kiss was sweet.
No gilded walls were there, no lofty dome,
But love's divine inscription—" HOME, SWEET HOME."

　　But, now, still more complete,
Thy higher home !　In God's sublimest sense ;
Enduring, perfect, blissfulness intense ;
For all our toils heaven's royal recompense,
　　Where all the Christly meet.
The jasper walls are there, and splendor's dome,
　The Father's House ! Home, sweeter, SWEETEST HOME!
1895.

THRESHOLD.

OPEN wide the palace gates,
　　On the threshold patience waits ;
Then the spirit cleansed from sin,
Robed in white, shall enter in ;
Sword unbuckled, cross laid down,
We shall wear the victor's crown.

1894.

OLD—NEW.

　　The old develops new,
Like bursting buds from Aaron's withered rod,
Or a white lily from the cold black sod,
Like sweet fresh life, from the warm heart of God :
　　Like morning's pearly dew
On the dry grass, flashing beneath the skies,
So from the old, new dispensations rise,
And truths evolve, Christ-hued, each a divine surprise.

1894.

THE ROYAL CROWN.

HIGHEST bestowment ! Coronation day !
　　Infinite condescension, God comes down,
Here by the matchless sea, in his grand way,
　　And on our work places his royal crown ;
And honored thus, before his throne we fall,
　　For God alone is Great ! He, the ETERNAL ALL !

1894.